I0098055

READER VIEWS
Bronze
2021
REVIEWERS CHOICE AWARDS

Echoes From The Wind

H.T. Manogue

In Memory Of Beezie
1930-2020

Other Works by H. T. Manogue

Poetry

Short Sleeves: A Book for Friends 2006 Collection

Short Sleeves: A Book for Friends 2007 Collection

Short Sleeves Spirit Songs 2008 Collection

Essays

Short Sleeves Insights: 2010 Collection – Out of Print

Novels

Living Behind the Beauty Shop

2011

The Butterfly Ball

2012

Bed Bosh & Beyond

2013–2014

Black Orchid Night

2015

Pine Cone Pandemic

2019

Copyright 2020, H. T. Manogue
All Rights Reserved

Echoes From The Wind
ISBN- 0-9778130-9-6
ISBN-13: 978-0-9778130-9-4

www.echoesfromthewind.com
www.shortsleeves.net
http://www.halmanogue.blogspot.com

A Poetry Toast
To
Kathleen Jacoby

Kathleen Jacoby was a writer's writer. Kathleen's consciousness disengaged from mass reality in 2019.

I first met Kathleen when I had the itch to share my form of poetry with the world. One of my submissions found its way to Kathleen when she was the editor of Children of the New Earth Magazine. Kathleen published a couple of my poems in that ahead-of-its-time magazine.

When I got the urge to write novels, Kathleen graciously read my manuscripts. She was a gifted author and an accomplished essayist. After she read my work, she would offer feedback that gifted authors give. For thirteen years, Kathleen's inspiration kept me on my writing road. At times, I would zig and zag on that road, but she always found a way to make sense of my thoughts. Her comments stimulated my resolve to write about topics that don't fit the norm. Her open mind, creative skills, and editing prowess gave people the gifts she wanted to give. Kathleen spread positive energy in a delightful four-dimensional way of knowing. People around the world continue to experience her energy by visiting her website.

Kathleen Jacoby was an editor, columnist, numerologist, and author of Vision Of The Grail: A Spiritual Journey at the Dawn of the 21st Century. Kathleen was also the editor of The Inner Voice Magazine.

Kathleen's writing and thinking talents are on display here:

Seasons of the Soul: kathleenjacoby.blogs.com/seasonsofthesoul/

Deep Bow To Graphic Artist Jess Galbraith

Jess created the cover of Short Sleeves Insights in 2007,
so when I needed help developing the shortsleeves.net website,
I called Jess. She also provided the expertise I needed to get
Pine Cone Pandemic ready for publication. And she helped publish this book.

Jess calls herself a graphic designer, but I call her creativity at its best.

For more information about Jess and her email her at: leedesign@leedesign.org

Poet's Note

Rummaging through years of self-help, psychology, religious teachings, and poetry books, I discovered a common thread. Finding value in myself started with finding out who I really was. It turns out I am many selves expressing my ever-changing belief system at various points in linear time. For years, I acted and thought in distinct ways to fit in or try to control and dominate situations and people in order to achieve some sort of value-fulfillment. The self writing this book is a different self who expresses beliefs, social stigmas, physical life, as well as non-physical life, in an unorthodox way.

You'll notice every word has a capital crown in my work. I do that to show every word in my poetry is an expression of the poetry it helped create. Each word deserves the respect and the dignity it earned being a whole part of the whole thought.

The poetry in this book comes from my collaboration with my non-physical energy personality.

HTM

April 2020

Front and Back Cover
Compliments Of
International Acclaimed Artist
Paul Harmon

I've been a Paul Harmon fan for almost 30 years. My first encounter with Paul came in the form of a plate he painted and donated to an auction. Joanie and I happened to be at that auction, and we won a piece of American art history. We became the proud owners of an original plate with Paul's face on it. I told Joanie any painter who would paint his face on a plate certainly had Picasso and Matisse consciousness in their DNA.

Paul is one of those people who live in multiple worlds at the same time. His work reflects those worlds. Every artist would like to dash off to Paris and be part of the Paris art scene. And Paul did that. He spent more than eleven years in Paris. The Museum of the Principality of Monaco, and the city of Caen, France found the beauty, creativity, and the salient messages in Paul's work too good to pass up. But Paul's museum-quality work is also on display in the Tennessee State Museum, the George Bush Presidential Library, and Museum, and the Tampa Museum of Art.

The list of awards Paul has hanging somewhere in his memory is impressive by anyone's standards. His quick wit, compassionate being, and energetic artistic flair are hard to do anything with, but bathe yourself in them. Paul has that "I've known you for years' country charm," so it's charming to be in his company. The secret to Paul's amazing ability to turn thoughts into tangible things is on display when you spend a little time with him.

I finally met Paul a couple of years ago. We knew some of the same people, and we both had stories to share. Sitting in an artist's studio feeling like Van Gogh would jump out of the bathroom any moment was certainly an adrenaline rush. Paul's studio was alive with paintings, paint, and memorabilia. Our chats always ended in a zone of grateful remembering. That's where Paul likes to hang out when he's not creating another masterpiece that the Linkster Generation will admire, collect, and pay dearly for.

Paul's front cover painting from his Her Face Series shows the emotional diversity in my poetry.

Paul's back cover painting Essay About Landscape captures the pensive mood of the book.

For more Paul Harmon information visit: paulharmon.com

You are about to experience a group of thoughts joined in poems.
These thoughts move past the boundaries created by our belief systems.
The energy within each boundless thought expands a kite of awareness
that freely floats in a mixture of value-fulfillment,
energy transformation, spontaneity,
and creativity .

My life's blossom might have bloomed on all sides
Save for a bitter wind which stunted my petals
On the side of me which you in the village could see.
From the dust I lift a voice of protest:
My flowering side you never saw!
Ye living ones, ye are fools indeed
Who do not know the ways of the wind
And the unseen forces
That govern the processes of life.

Spoon River Anthology
Edgar Lee Masters

And Write All The Wrongs In Dynamic Tension
With Pen That Wanders Through Poetry's Pension.
Black And White Thoughts Gather In Exquisite Manifestations
That Fill A Void With Miraculous Temptations.
Singed With Art Of Self Appreciation
Word After Word Describes
Essence In Creation.

Singed

A Canopy of Thinking
Brings Consciousness Together In Verse.
The Poet Moves In Expanding Awareness As
Each Metaphor Dances With Explicit Expression.
Ancient Mysteries Explode In Honorable Mention
As Poets Dig Into Another Dimension.

A Canopy Of Thinking

Beliefs Inject Life With Perceptions.

Choices Fulfills Thoughts With Manifestations.

A Self Supports An Ocean Floor Of Consciousness.

As Thoughts Create Physical Illusions.

Language Is Expression Of Vibrations.

In Probable Realities, Time Has Unlimited Dimensions

Within Endless Dimensions Of Spacious Consciousness.

Beliefs

I'm Voting Today.
I'm Voting For Self-Love.
My Inner Self-Love.
I'm Casting My Vote For Connection.
My Inner Connection.
The Connection I Know Intuitively.
It's Not A Partial Connection
Filled Fabricated Truths.
And It's Not Someone Else's
Love Of Conformity.

I'm Voting Today

The Wind Grabs Me
I Rest On A Breeze Of Peace
Moving With Its Gentle Motion
I'm Dressed In My Suit Of Fall
Ready To Meet My Maker
And Return To The Oneness Of Me
Being A Leaf
On An Ever-Expanding
Tree Of Life

The Wind Grabs Me

Being A Thought

Flowering Abundantly

A Psychic Sunset Blooms

A Psychic Sunset Blooms

Cracked Bells
Ring
In The Chapel
Of Pain
Hearing
Only
The Echo
Of
The Ringer

Pain

Moving Through Experiences
With The Force Of Consciousness
Brings Time To A Moment
Where All Love And Lovers Exist.
Embracing Intense Diversity,
The Lovers Rejoice
In Creative Synchronicity.
Dressed In Heat-Filled Synchronicity,
Lovers Capture Time In Moments Of Allowance,
And Toast Another Year.

Moments Of Allowance

Just To Be A Leaf
Floating Thru The Breeze
Landing Anywhere
Without A Care
Consciousness Dares
To Take Me There
Simple Prayer
Branch Is There
In Mind's Laird

Just To Be A Leaf

The Bowels Of Wasteful Blokes
Shady Puddles Of Disdain
Gives Indifference A Shot Of Influence.
Marching Masks Pass The Test When
Noxious Notions Capture Civility
And Blur The Law With Slaveries Glam.
That's A Wretched Trap
Soaked In Dreadful Sap.

Dreadful Sap

Spin Like A Spoke Or Ride Like A Bloke.
Energy Splits Hair It's Not A Dare.
To See Your Self As The More Than Two.
Independence Screams
Consciousness Dreams
Numbers Don't Drift But Fragments Do.

Fragments Do

Chocolate Roses Drip With Fragrance.
Mint Laced Thoughts Melt Into A Creamy Reality.
Spicy Melodies Float On Clouds Of Freedom.
Bubbling Friendships Unite In The Bottle Of Time.
Tender Memories Swim In The Waters Of Now.
Delicious Dreams Sizzle In The Drizzle Of Polarity.
As Future Rides On The Back Of Epistemology.

Epistemology

A Code Of Silence Tests The Walls Of Freedom.
Tattered Beliefs Slip Through Partisan Clouds
As Aspects Of Those Beliefs Dance In Rhombic Disorder
Looking For A Right Angle.

A Code Of Silence

Time For Birthday Rhymes.
Night Owl Paints
To The Beat Of Paris Time.
Pick A Treat. They All Speak.
Color Explodes. Naked Knows. In One Stroke,
Creativity Glows.
Nashville Bake. Butterfly's Skate.
While Artist Soaks In Copious
Canvas Cakes.

Canvas Cakes

To: Paul Harmon

Friendship Sea Land Of Glee
Yearning To Be Heard.
Timeless Religion Hidden Wisdom
Consciousness Wrench Has Conviction Frets.
Arrant Veneer's Tyranny's Beer.
Animal Matter Picks Its Power In
Restless Wakes While Waves Shake.
Tribalism's Charm Is Well Worn
When Afflicted Tongues Start To Gloat
On Color-Coded Boxes Where Feral Friendship
Takes A Vote.
Racist Beat Has No Feet Cause
The Promise Land Band Has First Seat.

Racist Beat

Space Explodes. Birth Chimes.
Mental Ditches Have Experience Glitches.
Dust Off The Blinds Time's End Game
Is Up In Flames.

A World Of Wonder Tightens Its Load.
What To Gain Bowels Shiver
Space Takes Paint Time Explains
From Canvases We Create.

Space Takes Paint

Bad To The Bone
Wacky Dicks Stand Alone.
Gromits Tight, Dick Feels Right.
Wrester's Delight, Justice Fright.
Party's Goo's A Hungry Chew.
Pull The Bone Bluebirds Moan
With Constitutional Threads Now Thee Wed
A Blue-Red Stew Has Gaul In View.
Time To Chug, Bar The Bugs
Cock And Bull Look Good On You.

Wrestlers Delight

Schumpeter Got It Right
Jackass Stew Is A Nasty Brew
One Sip Will Do.
Banana Peels Hearts That Squeal.
Mick's Action, Brown Keeps Crashing
While Twisted Sister Sniffs Ancestral Glue.

The Planet's Rock. Earthquake Bashes Satisfaction
All That Matters Doesn't Matter.
In A Minute, Coin's Stuck In It.
Eloquent Lips To Lick
Perception Flips In Bloody Sips.

Bloody Sips

I Am A Tree If I Want To Be.
Standing Tall Or Not At All.
Turning Green To Make A Scene
Or Just As Red With Things Unsaid.
An Ants Retreat. A Worm's Warm Bed. A Bird's Delight
With Birth In Sight.
An Owl's Call When Night Befalls,
Or On A Branch Where Music Pranced.
Trees Are Magic When They Dance.

When They Dance

Intense Diversity Guides Me Through the Contrast Of Being Physical.
A Non-Physical Self Celebrates Each Physical Creation.
Without Conditions Or Judgments.
Dressed In Legacy Scent Of Order,
Experiences Dip Themselves
In A Psychologically Mixture Of Humanity
That Illuminates The Spontaneous Force Within Me.

Spontaneous Force

Connected Brushes Of Energy
Paint A Picture Of Reality.
Each Brush Mixes Its Own Reality
With Thought-Filled Deep-Rooted Strokes.
A Bubbling Brew Of Color And Race
Rises To The Surface
Yearning To Be Whole Within The
Whole
That Presents Itself
To Itself
In A Blind Display
Of Awareness.

Blind Display Of Awareness

Standing On The Edge Of A Moment
I Backflip Into A World
Where Time And Space
Collect The Debris
Of The Past.
As This Me Moves Through Sundays
I Sense A Me Within Me.
And This Me
Is Many Me's
Living Simultaneously
In Deconcentrated Channels
Of Moments.

Channels Of Moments

Evolution Of Consciousness
Is An Inner Universal Law Of Attraction.
Mind Has No Form But Shapes A Brain.
Space Has No Form But Seats A Universe.

Life Has Twin Flames
That Ignite A Thought.

Truth Deals In Value
Durability, Spontaneity,
And
Energy Transformation.

Evolution Exists For Expansion
Nothing Is Left To Death
But The Duality
Of Separation.

Consciousness Survives Itself.
Evolution Repeats Itself.
I Digest A Self
And Truth
Repeats On Itself.

Evolution

Moon Leaps From A Jar
Covered In Bees.
Another Moon Drips In Carmel Licking Lips Of Silence.
A Moonlit Shadow Of Oceans
Wanders Through Yesterday
Caught In A Milky Way
With Nothing
But Threads Of Consciousness
To Smile About.

To Smile About

The Crusty Fog Of Decadence Had A Plan.
Augustus Had One Too.
Spuriously Fragile, Foolishly Intoxicated
Ego's Contrivance Rushed In On Waves Of Glut.
While Tongue Lashing Got The Partisans Flu
From Bleeding Scars Fertilizing The Zoo.
Confounding Petulance Compliments Of Orange-Filled Poo.
Void Of Equal Measures, Red, White, And Blue Sat In Catabolic Hysteria
While The Crusty Fog Of Decadence Taught The Scars
A Thing Or Two.

Bleeding Scars

Church Of Sin Look Within.
Hounds Of Winter Children Of Never
Are Addicted To Time Nursery Rhyme.
Wake Up Bugs Got No Time.
Conflicted Groups Screwed The Pooch.
Plato Knew Fear Grows Balls.
Courageous Minds Stand Tall When
The Hounds Of Winter
Meet The Children Of Never
And Mellow Out The Brawl.

The Brawl

Wants Need Desire's Action.
Thornier Thoughts Need Action Too.
Build A Bear Paint Silver Hair
Doo-Whop Becomes A Part Of You.
Emotional Gas. Turpentine Past.
Perception Roll, Action Bowls
With Conjured Gas In A Trance.
Dreams Love Romance Too.

Conjure Gas

Monarch Fever
Knarly Beavers Those Political Cleavers
Bury The Oceans Charm The Snakes
Democracy Prays
Capitalistic Maze Has Social Days.
Rusty Brains Go Insane
Smash A Mountain Cordelia Pain
Is In Ignorance's Game.

Capitalistic Maze

If A Universe Was A Painting,
Black Takes The Spotlight
Energy's Action Tops The Show.
Consciousness Colored Inner Tricks
Kick Into Over Time
As Thoughts Ride Tides And
Differences Dab The
Corners Of Its Self.

If The Universe Was A Painting

High Blood Fever Low Life Shivers
Umbilicus Feathers Stick Together
When Planet Rocks Roll And Twist.
Hardcore Power Makes Earth Crumble.
Wake Up Time. Monocot Motion Does The Locomotion.
Surf Gets Raucous While Boats Look For Overtime.
Ants Stumble. Mountains Go For Broke.
Wasps Mumble Awareness Looks Good On You
It Don't Matter Grab A Cab Flag A Crab
Water Took First In Crew.

Ants Stumble

Seas Of Doubt Yearn For Splendor.
Father's Glory Tells No Story
When Coin Delights And Freedom Fights
To Save Its Inner Glue.
Build The Walls Stack The Benches
Constitutional Questions Fog Perceptions
When Judges Drink A Baneful Brew.

Baneful Brew

There Is No Shame In Your Game
Animal Instinct Got To Peel
The Tribal Ritual From The Real.
Sinners Spin. Thoughts Cracks A Grin
Undertow Wedge Mindset Shot
Man Can't Win With Bags Of Sin.
Psychic Masks Parade in Casts
That Color The Psychic Stew

Psychic Stew

Feminine Side My Oh My,
Minute Came Quick Pogo Stick.
Thistle For Your Thoughts.
Time to Gloat. Seeds To Spare
With Urban Hair. What A Dare!
Balls On Fire Got To Vote.
That's Flavor Town's
Ghostly Roast.

Ghostly Roast

You're In The Desert A Taste Of Justice Godly Style
A Bit Of Pain Sweaty Gain
When Precocious Gods Sit And Wait
In Credence's Place.
Now Meet The Snakes
Waiting To Take The Bait
While Planets Dance In Place.
It's A Pettifog Gait Patently Designed
With Scraps Of Shade And No Time.
Fulminating Bonfires, In Bellicose Dreams Preacher Screams
Oceanic Sweat A Scurrilous Treat
When Plants Dig Swaying To That Inner Beat.

Inner Beat

Symbiotic Fluid How'd You Do It?
Rhetoric Bear, Religious Stare.
Mercy Had No Clue Dependency Rules The Crew.
Arrogant Curse Bible Verse.
Ancient Hearse Has Life Immersed In
Demagogue Fame That Underbelly Pain
While Rank Weed Voices Mixes Choices.
Dig The Band, Toss in Sand.
The Human Flu
Got A Hold On You.

Symbiotic Fluid

The Backside Of The Law Started Circling The Drain.
Its Orange Colored Rumpster
Made The Elephants Dare To Bear
The Comedic Notes Of Worthy Hares
That Run In Tandem With Blank Stares.

The Ego-Stroking Rumpster Has A Midas Touch
That Wiggles And Screams As A Herd Of Jacks
Split Hares And Break Themselves In Two.

But The Backside Of The Law Keeps Circling The Drain
Dripping A Homegrown Mixture And A Nasty Stench
From A Rumpster Filled With Mobster Mensch.

Circling The Drain

Consciousness
That Psychic Honey Pot Of Godly Style
Whips Up A Cell-Created Brew.
Fluid Deuces Dipped In Creative Juices Dance
With Starlight Sass And Abstractive Gas.
While Conformity Dreams And Spontaneity Screams
La La Land Has High Beams.

La La Land

Judgmental Stench Lingers In Cemetery Row.
Toxic Air, Thoughts Are Prayers. Moments Are Free
In Freedom's Face. Worship Knows Judgment Crows
In Ignorant Fields Of Glory.
While Brilliant Rays Of Parrot Proper Nonchalance
Whips Thoughts Into A Physical Stew

Physical Stew

Addicted To Time Nursery Rime
The Hounds Of Winter Children Of Never
The Church Of Sin Look Within.
Energy Kisses Time And Space
While Birth Takes A Seat
That Touches The Light Where Love Is
All We Really Know.

Really Know

Orange Bird Tangles With Yellow Bird
Yellow Bird Tells Rooster War Is The Way To Go.
But Orange Bird Told The Brown Bird
Arrogance And Ignorance Give The Cemetery
A Chance To Grow.
Blackbird Took A Shot To Make White Bird Glow.
Then Blackbird Went Nesting Covered In Game
Waiting For The Time Orange Bird Remembers
Ignorant Awareness Starts Wisdom's Game

Ignorance Awareness

Bodies Have No Boundaries
Health Is Up To You.
Pine Cone Prominence Has The Key.
Paddlefish Dance, Million-Year Romance
But Yangtze's Plan Blew The Beast
While History Melts In Two.
Formal Dance, Needle Romance.
Pine Cone Magic Changes The Beat
And Lets The Soul Take First Seat.

Pine Cone Magic

I Can Be That Endless Cloud.
That Puff Of Consciousness
Filling Itself
With Other Consciousness.
I Am Action
In A Puff Of Consciousness.
And A Pearl In The Oyster
Of Eternity.

A Puff Of Consciousness

Thoughts Covered In Ice
Get Seedy And Messy When Noble Gestures,
Guarded Treasures Are Too Sick To Pop The Top
Or Take A Leap On Winds That Bubble
When Trouble Captivates The Mind.

Pose Nude Planets Do
Let Desires Swoon
While Balloons Blow Mankind
With Nursery Rhythms

Nursery Rhythms

I Choose When And How I Want Angels Toast.
The Toast My Inner Personality Already Knows
In A Multidimensional Consciousness Way.
Perceptions Of Separation Swing
From The Cobwebs Of Contrast
In A Factious Display Of Unity
While The Wings Of Angels
Toast The Fiction
With Remembrance

Angels Toast

Magnificent Tree Enlighten Me.
Consciousness Of Beauty
Instantaneously Translation
Bark's A Home, But Doesn't Groan.
Roots Want A Show.
Leaves Want Glow.
Sum Of Its Parts— Eccentric Art
Relish-Free Diversity.
In Nature's Arc.

Relish Free Diversity

The Silence Is the Vibration Of Another Realtiy.
A Reality Filled With The Essence Of A Cricket's Voice
In Every Moment.
Listening To The Essence Of Silence Within Action Wrapped Moments
I Hear The Cricket's Voice
In Me

Cricket's Voice

The Wind Rides In On Cold Shoulders.
A Wiskful Scent Of Love Lingers
Between The Alley Of Moments.
Cold Shoulders Light A Storm Of Plenty
As The Wind Stings The Ages
With Tattered Dreams And Cold Places,
That Once Harbored Love
Between Momentous Alleys.

Momentous Alleys

A Tear From The Eye Of Love
Turns A River Of Sorrow Into An Ocean Of Joy.
A Smile From The Face Of Love
Moves Mountains Of Frowns
Into A Valley Of Peace.
A Kiss From The Mouth Of Love
Makes Angels Dance With Delight.
Love Makes Us Love Ourselves
In The Mirror Of Moments.

Mirror Of Life

Buddha There You Stand.
Sending Emails On Your Energy Trail.
That Guiding Light Monk Day Bright
Heart Of Joy, Soul Of Toys.
Abundance Spreader, Awareness Blender Wrapped In An
Absorbing Sponge With Frugal Suffer-Less Dust.
Fork Of Peaceful Thoughts. Knife That Humanity Trusts
Your Forgiveness Spoon Kicks The Self-Hate Race
In Its Face.
Forward Pace That No-Thing Place
Where Suzuki Got A Taste

Suzuki Got A Taste

Silently Drifting In A Blue Print Of Always
I Transpose My Self.
My Wafer Thin Sensitivity
Discovers Consciousness Floating In Soggy Memories.
I Drip In Complexity While Reaching For A Beach Towel.
Waist Deep Beliefs Linger In Muddy Always.
Thoughts Become Neck-Deep
In The Precious Presence Of Always.
Ever-Changing Clouds Of Consciousness Attract
Thought's Beauty In Transformable Energy
That Compliments Itself.

Ever-Changing Clouds

I Paint In Fragments That Change In Contrast.
I Move From Canvas To Canvas
Expressing The Desire To Be A Conscious Painting Of Inner Consciousness.
My Ink Well Of Acceptance Dries In The Air Of Separation.
My Brush Dips Itself in Blood
As Mental Enzymes Turn Into Human Thoughts
Copied From Energy's Unique Display Of Awareness.
My Outer Edges Drizzle With Magical Desires.
Fresh Beliefs Become Vibrations Of Expression
And My Nucleus Colorfully Entertains
A Family Of Nuances
That Shade Themselves In Dreams.
An Art Form Of Timeless Motion
Another Self Captures My Multiplicity
In Free Style, And I Rest
On An Easel Of Eternity.

A Conscious Painting

Fragments Moving From Canvas To Canvas
Belt Vibrational Tones Deep In The Moments
Of Color.
Action Creates Another Fragment
Seeping Through Bundles Of Complexity
With Artful Spontaneity.
Energy's Conscious Family Has Abstract Conformity's
Framework Running Through Its DNA.

Abstract Conformity

Thoughts Smacked Belief In The Gut.
Subjectivity Took That Experience
By Its Tale As Another Teflon-Coated Memory
Has Objectivity Oozing From Conflicted Veins.
Battered Beliefs Took Another Knee-Bender
When A Gaggle Of Thoughts Run Free Giving Birth To Other Beliefs.
Energy Regenerators Within Black Holes
Give The Gaggles New Life.

Black Holes

Ancient Chi Tangos Through Us.
Connected Thoughts Rumba Like Cells
Percolating In A DoWop Pool Of Excitement.
Internal Bubbles Bounce In Tandem
Within Moments As Fabricated Veins Of Gold
Display Their Handiwork In The Foam Of Perceptions.

The Foam Of Perceptions

Cascading Bubbles Of Consciousness
Float Through Time In A Stream Of Solitary.
Multiplicity's Waves Of Energy
Wash Sullen Stones From The Bottomless Apex
Of Aphotic Aphorism.
Aphonic Aphids Suck In Wisdom.
Apathetically Apatite's Blossom In Colorful Crystal Symmetry.
As Apocalypse Of Apologists Wipe Apolitical Sweat From Apostasy.
Aposiopesis Lingers, While An Apo Geotropic Thought
Captures Water's Dimensionality

Bubbles Of Consciousness

In The Silence Of Being I See You
Floating Through The Essence Of Age.
Your Infinite Grace Showers My Senses
With A Forgotten Dream.

Your Infinite Softness Gently Touches
My Awareness As I Awaken
To The Voice Of Energy's Twitch.

There I Find The Real Age.
There I Sense.
There I Am.
As You Are,
In Love.

As You Are

A Self Is Found
In Each Belief In Each Moment
In Each Experience.

A Self Is Energy Completely A Glow
Fueled By The Match
Of Consciousness.

Burning At Different Intensities
The Flame Of Each Self
Becomes A Candle Within The Framework
Of Spontaneous Selves.

The Self Is A Reflection Of Becoming The Wick
Candle, And Light.

A Self

The Rocky Ledge Has New Life.
Yesterday's Beauty Blooms Again
In Another Version Of Its Own Consciousness.
Similar Petals Express Vivid Colors With Fresh Candor
And Wisdom.

Wind Blown Artisans Move Freely But Never Leave Their Spot
Of Inception.
The Scent Of Nectar Beckons Life Enticing
Gift Of Awareness.
A Sunset Introduces An Energy Filled Sky.
Each Particle Of Action Adorns A Shiny Crown.

Stillness Speaks In Harmony. Roots Drink In Gratitude.
Stems Dress In Simplicity Waiting For Nothing, But
Experiencing Everything, As A Flower Blooms In The Complete
Action Of Its Own Consciousness.

A Flower Blooms

I Hear An Atom Vibrating In Its Own Consciousness.
The Center Has The Roar Of Massiveness
In Its Tiny Reality.
Constantly Creating An Impetus Of Change
The Known Is The Knower
The Seer Speaks Of Seeing The Unseen.
Manifestation Rises In Fusion.
Combustion Creates Form In The Thickness Of Time.
I Hear An Atom Talking Bout The Weather Of Synchronicity
And
I Feel A Drop Of Awareness,
Continuously.

Continuously

Twisting Through The Aggressive Rubble
A Crazy Thought Becomes A Belief In Magical Motion.
Fumbling Around Space A Crazy Tool Bag
Becomes History.
Crazy Psychic Magnets Attract Energy In A Congress
Filled With Matter Less Energy.
Blank Shelves Carry A Crazy Carcass As
Stocks Ask Wall Street For A Spoon.
Insurance Dips Into Empty Pockets Of Ethics
As Crazy Bankers Step On Their Own Tales
Crying Balance Now Due.
A Collection Of Socialists Find Peace Crazy
On The Steps Of Kat Man Due.
Crazy Ice Melts In Daylight.
War Jumps Over The Moon Landing.
Torrent Gardens Of Craziness
Birth Reconstruction.

Crazy Psychic Magnets

Dancing In A Dream
I Become A Madman Dressed In A Divine Question.

Answers Slip Into Majestic Enzymes Of Consciousness
That Slowly Drip With My Essence.

Innately, I Touch My Oneness As Twinkling Stars
Burst With Energy.
Captured In Exotic Energy
My Dream Becomes Reality.

Dancing

I Remember You
You Warm Breeze That Twists My Hair
On A Salty Beach.
A Star Filled Galaxy Sparkling
In Its Own Image.
Thoughts That Bend And Wiggle
Like A Stream Of Crystal Clear
Moon Water.
I Remember The You That I Long To Be.
The Dust That Does Not Stir.
The Water That Is Born From
Its Off Springs.

Off Springs

Eclipsing Through Myself
I Feel Consciousness Exploding Into Atoms.
With Wings Of Awareness
I Touch My Soul Through The Peephole Of Peculiarity.
Squinting To See The Fibers Of Infinity
Meshed Together In A Complex System Of Non-Verbal Symmetry,
I Transform My Thoughts Into Imagery
Surrounded By Selves.
I Move Freely From Reality To Reality With Graceful Originality.
I Touch My Senses With Innate Simplicity, And Limitless Modality
While I Project My Self In A Never Ending Magnetic Bubble Called Life.

Magnetic Bubble

Words Are Energy

They Vacillate In Formlessness.

Singed Words Dangle On Participles Of Linear Time Then Manifest As Emotions.

Historic Words Hide In A Grain Of Sand As Sea Water's Memory Drips Into Forgot-
ten Footprints.

A Fearful Sentence Becomes An Iceberg Locked In A Frozen Paragraph Of
Thoughts.

Sliding Off A Cliff Of Senseless Words, A Crack Of Thunder Signals
Its Distortion In An Energetic Display Of Consciousness.

Satellites Signal Emptiness As A Galaxy Trips On Static Sentences
Filled With Slippery Intrusive Words In A Comet
Made Of Metaphors.

Comet Made Of Metaphors

Flowers Of Energy Bloom
In Silent Beauty
In Seed-Filled Contemplation

Flowers

In Truth, Fragrance Lingers Much Longer Than Words.
Color Vibrates In Scented Tones Of Awareness.
A Rhapsody Of Aromas Float Majestically In Ornate Cylinders
Of Changing Mental Enzymes.

As Space Drips Into A Forgotten Hourglass Filled With Realities
I Wander Endlessly Sensing Your Definitive Consciousness
As Material Sounds Tap On My Mind With Diluted Verse.

Captured In Perfumed Desires But Drowning In Anthropomorphic Beliefs
Babbling Matter Drenches My Synchronicity
While My Harmonic Silence Swims In Awareness.

Harmonic Silence

Just Some Of You Lingers On My Senses
A Fragrance Of Lavender
Laced With Jasmine
Swirls Through My Mind
Just Some Of You
Squeezes Through The Crack
In My Belief Ridden Lips And
I Taste My Freedom.
Just Some Of You Embraces My Memory Of You,
And I Realize Just Some Of You
Knows The Sum Of Me.

Just Some Of You

Love Songs Drip In the Winds Of Consciousness
Tethered To An Army Of Molecules.
Cells Move Through Endless Realities.
Each Cell Listens As
Echoes Rumble Through Breathless Words.
But With Thoughts Transfixed I Solve The Glitch.
Dig The Joy. Cells Are Coy,
But They Do Make Noise.

Cells Are Coy

A Grain Of Sand Moves Through Time Creating A Floor Of Life.
Each Spec Waits For The Tide To Twirl And Propel It Majestically
In An Undercurrent Of Perceptional Intentions.
Colors Washed In The Taste Of Antiquity
Scooped In The Bucket Of Psychic Bed Rock.
Shovels Of Dreams Dig Through Choices,
As One Grain Of Time Turns Imagination
Into A Beach Of Choices.

Beach Of Choices

Crow Sitting On A Heap Of Trash. Crow Can't Take It.
Crows Been Told Only White Got Cash Black's Gotta Be The Trash
In A Pot Where Wolves Deal Hash
Just To Make A Dime And Drain Some Brin.
Crows Sitting On A Heap Of Trash. Crow Took The Hard Road
As White Walked The Racial Plank.

Crows Sitting

Inner Counterparts Coded In Twisted DNA
Pose Nude And Cross Planes Of Reality,
And Exist In Multidimensional Personifications.

Deep Messages Come Freely Without Form.
Focused Vibrations Deliver Blueprints Simultaneously
In Vibrational Tones Between Planes Of Reality
Where Multiple Selves Take Their Course In Awareness.

Multiple Selves

Dancing Particles
Samba To The Beat
Of Creation.
Minds Move In Shadows
As Energy Re-Shapes Itself.
Mystical Friendships Bond In No Space
And Memories Become The Now.

Dancing Particles

Election Blues How Do You Do?
Kiss A Mirror Turn With Grace
Reflection Shines In That Face.
Top Of The Season Appreciation Mission.
Kiss An Ocean. Take A Dip
Bathe In Synchronicity
On This Trip.

This Trip

Salvation Sits On An Altar In Robes Of Sin.
Religious Thoughts Drap Yesterday's Separation In Ancient Symbols.
Vibrating Tones Heal Controlling Perceptions.
Colored By Addicts Treating Addicts.
Singed By The Fire Of Guilt
Toothless Time
Creates Impressive Mysteries.

Toothless Time

Will There Really Be A Morning If Life Is Filled With Gray?
Will There Really Be A Day If Life Is Dues To Pay?
Will There Really Be A Sunrise If All I Do Is Pray?
Will There Really Be Tomorrow
When A Morning Sits In Clay?

Morning!

Family Trance Uncles And Aunts
Santa Wears Baggy Pants.
Holiday Wishes Energy Kisses
Love's Our Music Man.
Credit Card Stew Destiny's Flu.
Overboard Shuffle Candy Coated Truffles
Life's Inner Brew Is Calling You.
Another Tree God Bless Thee.
In a Haze New Year's Rage.
Black Eyed Peas Power Seeds
Harmony Bees Are Calling, "Please."
Mental Notes Hearts That Soak Physical Matter's Overactive Bladder.
Glory Be Enlightened Me. Time Is Clear Change Is Here Drumming To The Beat
Of Love's Music Man While The Family Trance Turns Into A Yearly Dance.

Family Trance

Soaring Within Me
A Voice Whispers
Creating Tiny Teardrops
That Fill
A Silent Void

Silent Void

Quietly, I Find Myself
Lost In A Thought.
A Dream Rescues Me
And I Become Nothing
But Shapeless Aware
Consciousness.

Quietly

Raging Currents Create Bubbles Of Consciousness.
Silent Energy Expresses Itself In Interlocking Geometric Shapes.
Enzymes Build Bridges Of Matter. A Plump Posture
Of Psychic's Flexible Bubbles Drift In Tandem
Through Focused Thoughts Floating Gracefully Through
Non-Physical Energy's Framework.

Focused Thoughts

Real Is A Room Where I Stand Wearing Nothing But My Self.
Real Is Just One Me In The House Of Multidimensionality.
I Feel The Sap Of Consciousness Stretch Within Me.
I Hear The Sounds Of Nature And Awaken From A Sleep.
I See The World Changing, And My Body Skips To The Beat.

Skips To The Beat

I Touch
A Sunburst Butterfly
And Feel Vibrational
Energy Resting
In The All Of Us.

Sunburst Butterfly

Non-Physical Energic Wind Dancers Circle Matter.
Streaming Awareness, What's The Matter?
Mind Clouds Play With Art.
Self-Rain Plays A Part.
Sprinkle A Little Gray Diversity's Colors Say.
Multiple Selves Take A Bow. Addiction Land Ego Grins
Has A High Tolerance For Buried Pleasures
And Psychic Treasures In
Those Inner Works Of Art.

Works Of Art

Nectar Of Unity Drips From Its Nothing.
I Dream Of Color, And Take The Trip.
A Moment In Multiplicity Swings From Consciousness
And Somersaults Into Being From Nothing But Myself.
Candidly Looking For A Complex Reality, Birth Races Towards A Second.
Drenched In Blue Green Responsibility Turquoise Metaphors Paint Me
On A Canvas Of Magnetic Energy Roots.

Magnetic Energy Roots

Fetus Focus Body Spat.
Consciousness Comes In Colors.
Fetus's Favor Is Consciousness Behavior
Clarity Of Purpose Is Built Within.

Fetus Focus

Forward Thoughts Reverse Themselves.
Twisted DNA Unravels
Strands Of Awareness.
Thought Cycles Rotate Cells.
It's A Penetrating Plan In Future's Band
It's Deliberate Vision In Eccentric Sand
While I March In Chromosome Land.

Chromosome Land

Remembering
Is
The
Vehicle
That
Takes Me
To
The Place
I
Have Always Been
And
Back Again.

The Vehicle

Mental Enzymes Drip Through Layers Of Consciousness
Coating Life With Inexhaustible Energy.
Being The Painter, I Become The Painting
Expressing Reality On An Easel Of Linear Time.
Drops Of Vibrant Colors Seep Through Floors Of Awareness
Capturing Mountains In A Mystic Mist
While Oceans Laugh At Apodictic Sunsets.
Earthly Shadows Cling To Speckled Ceremonious Dreams.
While Internal Blueprints, Laced In Multi-Colored Contradictions
Drenched Themselves In Bubbling Brushes.
My Life Is Brushy Highlights Shaded By
Ecliptic Pulsating Awareness Fill With
Charcoal Thoughts As My Energy Blinks.

Energy Blinks

Deep In The Canyons Of Consciousness
Families Dress Themselves In Enzymes.
Nothing Expands Into A Plethora Of Particles
That Encapsulate A Wave With Unfiltered Awareness.
A Force Filled Form Of Being Manifests Itself In Tandem With Molecules Dress As
Frigates Of Timelessness.
Elusive Probabilities Actively Dance In The Fertility Of The Moment.
Energy is Captured In Choices
As A Web Of Being Expands Within Abundance.
Focusing Water Drops Bounce Manifestations Off The Walls Of Remembering,
And They Free-Fall Into Primordial History.
Swallowing Another Reality, Entrenched In Its Own Juices, Existence Eats The
Cracker Of Immortality.
And Spits Out Another Blip Expressed As Conscious Consciousness.
Simultaneously Wisdom Speaks In Bilingual Silence
And The Self's Universal Echo Reaches Eternity.

Universal Echo

Simmering On The Stove Of Consciousness
A Light Flickers Beneath A Flame Filled With Connected Images.
Magnetic Movement Dangles From A Distorted Belief.
Myopic Influences Push Through A Collection Of Filtered Circumstances
Quietly Melting In A Stew Of Learning.
A Cryptic Reality Begins A Chaotic Rapture.
Pounds Frolic Through A Confused Pasture.
A Drop Of Awareness Drowns In Sweet Harmony.
Forming Crop Circles Leftover From
A Bleed-Through Identity
In Another Pot Of Reality.

Pot Of Reality

I Can Be The Rain And Listen To The Sound Of My Own Creations.
I Can Be The Stream And Capture The Sound Of Rain Drops
Expressing Themselves In Diversity.
I Can Be The River That Flows With The Energy Of The Forest.
I Can Be The Spirit Dancing With The Heartbeat Of The Universe
I Can Be An Ocean Of Sound That Echoes
Off Of All Consciousness
Within Me.

Within Me

It Seems Like You're Always There
Just A Breath Away
Whispering Softly
Gently Touching A Distant Memory
A Fragrant Field Of Consciousness
Blooms In Remembering

Remembering

Slowly I Awaken
Remembering Beauty Without Judgment
Grace Without Regret.
Splendor Without Remorse.
Candor Without Reprisal.
Cadence Without Restrictions.

Without Restrictions

Words Of Wisdom Seldom Listen To Themselves.
They Are Caught In The Throws Of Time.
Words Of Anger Seldom Hear The Cries Of Others
They Are Trapped In The Prison Of Fear.
Words Of Praise Seldom Fall On One's Self.
They Are Caught In Restlessness.
Words Of Freedom Seldom Release Themselves.
They Are Immersed In Lawlessness.
Words Of Gratitude Seldom Reveal Themselves.
They Are Transposed Into Helplessness.
Words Of Love Seldom Touch Others.
They Are Lost In The Disease Of Separation.

Seldom

Words Soak In Dreams,
Words Stuffed With Emotions Crawl
Through A Master Vine.
Words Of Power. Words Of Grace.
A Dualistic Race In Poetic Pace.
Words Are Maps. Words Are Traps Caught
In Time And Space
Within A Place Of Distorted Measures.

Distorted Measure

You Come To Me From A World Void Of Age
A World Colored In Vibrational Harmony.
A Match Stick Of Remembering
Singes My Senses.
I'm Capsulated By Your Golden Glow.
Your Essence Drips Through
The Crackless Memories That
Dance In Synchronicity, Speak In Tonality,
And Listen With Inter-Sensitivity's Ornamental Vision.
Compliments Of Conductive Subjectivity.

Conductive Subjectivity

Through My Consciousness I Connect To Love.
Through My Choices I Express Love.
Through My Probabilities I Experience Love.
Through My Separation I Remember Love.
Through My Pain I Test Love.
Through My Beliefs I Distort Love.
Through My Realities I Search For Love.
Through My Self I Forgive Love.
Through My Love I Become
A Symphony Of Conscious Love.

A Symphony

Offer Peace In Times Of No Peace.
Offer Understanding To Those Who Don't Understand.
Offer Healing To Those Who Have Misplaced Hope.
Offer Joy To All Who Give With Conditions.
Offer Love To All Who Love With Judgments.
Offer Appreciation
For All The Contrast And Diversity In Life.

Offer

Evolution Glue How Do You Do
Icy Crypt Got Heat's Trick.
Vexing Glamour Tom Cat Banner.
Tomorrow's Rake Begins To Flake.
Unknown Grins Comes From Within.
Yesterday's Romance That Body Slam Dance
Just Broke Out In Fins.

Body Slam Dance

The Coat Of Silence
Hangs On Freedom.
Tattered Beliefs Slip Through Aliquant Clouds.
Rants Of Consciousness
Rejoice In Nothingness.
As A Revolving Revue Of Unity
Dances with Rhombic Essence.

Rants Of Consciousness

There Is An Ethereal Presence In The Trees.

As The Wind Complements Their Consciousness.

Trees Speak A Language That Moves The Wind In

An Well-Orchestrated Silent Sonata.

A Leafonic Symphony Dripping In Esoteric Wisdom

Bends In Visceral Completeness.

While Their Roots

Begin Their Journey Inward.

Visceral Completeness

Philly Time Was Nursery Time
A Rolling Accordion Roast With Coffee Toast.
Dove Hums Matriarch's Tone Was Her Own
Her LifeLong Mate Like To Boast,
Family's First God Rehearsed.
Angels Grin That's A Win.

In The Silence, Nine Red Roses
Kissed The Freckled Dove.
It Was Spearmint Praise For The Days
When Bottle Caps In The Rain
Was The Only Pain.
Angel's Clue: The Doves Are Two
With God's Crew.

To: My McGann Family

A Poet's Journey

There's no denying it. My physical personality was lost in one crazy badass netherworld of misremembering for the first forty-seven years of my life. My inner personality was getting body-slammed by my physical one while I was building my egocentric world. I like to say I was a religious, capitalistic slave, immersed in a vat of distorted values. And here's the thing: that is a realistic description of the physical image I created through years of business conditioning and knee-jerk personal choices.

I was a hardheaded, egotistical college dropout with doctoral-level personality skills. My goal was to sell my way to fame and glory, one shoe at a time. I was a money-hungry young shoe salesman—a shoe salesman willing to do the low-class ego dance for an order. I had the capitalistic brazenness to move up the corporate shoe ladder. My capitalistic persona would always stretch reasonability to its outer limits. So when I failed a time or two or three, I blamed the system. But I rose from my self-created ashes and got objectively successful again by selling more than one shoe at a time. I was selling container loads of shoes at one time. And once I felt successful, I wanted more power and more recognition.

When I bet it all with a blundering, alcohol-enriched mind and threw my fun-loving talents on the shoe wolves, expecting to become one, my narrow-minded focus sent me over the cliff of self-discovery. My physical personality was in free fall, and all my lifelines burned in a fire I had made. My reality was changing, and I started to feel another presence within me. My four-dimensional personality was guiding me to the bottom so I could internally heal my self-imposed wounds. Once I hit bottom, my physical personality drifted in a mysterious mixture of self-pity and irrelevance. But my four-dimensional personality came to the rescue. My four-dimensional personality took over when my mother passed in 1996. And that personality helped me understand the passing of my younger brother, Bob, and my dad, Howard, in 2013. I felt something special during these monumental losses. It felt like I was standing in a nonphysical stream of understanding, and I felt the pure energy in that understanding.

My physical personality followed that stream when I began reading psychology and philosophy books. I found Rumi quotes in many of those books, so at forty-seven, I bought my first Rumi book. Rumi, the thirteenth-century Sufi mystic, is an inner-self shaker. I started to look at the nonphysical part of things because of Rumi. Then Confucius, Lao Tzu, Buddha, the German poet Rainer Maria Rilke, and the Englishman William Blake gave me their versions of inner personality expressions. Ralph Waldo Emerson, Ernest Holmes, James Allen, Jesus, Muhammad, and other soul-seekers through the ages all said the same thing. And they all used their inner personalities to say it. By the time I found Japan's Shinkichi Takahashi's work, I was on the edge of a nonphysical bridge. I realized that I'd been on that bridge all my physical life but had ignored being there. I'd always felt the presence of an agreeable being in my thoughts. But I rarely paid attention to that being until I read Ask and It Is Given as soon as it was published. Abraham, the author of the book, is a nonphysical energy personality who expresses commonsense thoughts about the nature of physical life. Then I hit the jackpot when I found the Seth Material. Jane Roberts, the poet and writer, brought the thoughts of nonphysical Seth into my world during my fifties. When Elias and Zurac came into my life in the first decade of the twenty-first century through the internet and a booth at Nashville's Galactic Expo, I realized that these nonphysical personalities' unfiltered messages were helping me forge an unfiltered path on this physical journey.

What I've learned on this journey is that I am here to physically experience my thoughts, emotions, and perceptions. I know now what the sages and the people who used their inner senses in this reality were trying to tell me and everyone else: Our thoughts and emotions are forms of energy that act like cells when we project them into our reality using a mechanism we call "perception." They are the tools we use to create what we experience physically.

I'm not here to form a group or write sermons about self-responsibility. And I'm not here to act like someone who crossed the self-awareness finish line and is basking in a state of bliss. My physical personality is still physically focused on creating my reality. But I'm increasingly using my inner personality to do it. I live a four-dimensional reality. And I'm just beginning to appreciate what that reality does for me.

www.ingramcontent.com/pod-product-compliance
Lightning Source LLC
Chambersburg PA
CBHW051733040426
42447CB00008B/1112